My Weird School FAST FACTS
Dinosaurs, Dodos, and Woolly Mammoths

Also by Dan Gutman

My Weird School
FAST FACTS
Dinosaurs,
Dodos, and
Woolly
Mammoths

Dan Gutman

Pictures by
Jim Paillot

HARPER
An Imprint of HarperCollinsPublishers

To Nina

The author gratefully acknowledges the editorial contributions of Nina Wallace.

Photo credits: Page 23: Robin2 / Shutterstock; 32: Michael Rosskothen / Shutterstock; 34: Michael Rosskothen / Shutterstock; 51: Craig Hanson / Shutterstock; 57: Dorling Kindersley / Getty Images; 57: Ryan M. Bolton / Shutterstock; 67: Herschel Hoffmeyer / Shutterstock; 72: Michael Rosskothen / Shutterstock; 76: Mark Garlick / Getty Images; 80: Warpaint / Shutterstock; 85: Nobumichi Tamura / Stocktrek Images / Getty Images; 93: EQRoy / Shutterstock; 98: legacy1995 / Shutterstock; 111: Linda Bucklin / Shutterstock; 137: Atomazul / Shutterstock; 149: W. Scott McGill / Shutterstock; 164: Mark 1260423 / Shutterstock; 168: Morphart Creation / Shutterstock; 176: BMJ / Shutterstock; 182: Zenobillis / Shutterstock; 184: Igor Matic / Shutterstock

My Weird School Fast Facts: Dinosaurs, Dodos, and Woolly Mammoths
Text copyright © 2018 by Dan Gutman
Illustrations copyright © 2018 by Jim Paillot

ISBN 978-0-06-267309-1 (pbk. bdg.) — ISBN 978-0-06-267310-7 (library bdg.)

18 19 20 21 22   CG/BRR   10 9 8 7 6 5 4 3 2 1

First Edition

Contents

The Beginning

 My name is A.J. and I _____ dinosaurs.

You have to fill in the blank in that sentence, because I'm not going to say the L word. Yuck! Disgusting! The L word is for girls, like Andrea Young, this annoying girl in my class with curly brown hair.

1

Well, *Andrea* has curly brown hair, not the class. A classroom doesn't have hair. It would be weird if a classroom had hair. Then our custodian, Miss Lazar, wouldn't have to mop the floor. She would have to *comb* the floor. Gross!

The point is, boys should never say the L word. That's the first rule of being a boy.

Where was I?

Oh yeah, dinosaurs.

Dinosaurs are supercool. Do you want to know why dinosaurs are supercool? Because they're superbig and superscary, but they're also super*dead*, so we don't have to worry about them chasing us down the street and biting our heads off. Ouch!

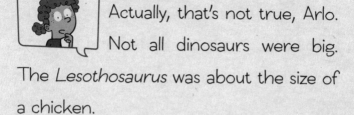

Actually, that's not true, Arlo. Not all dinosaurs were big. The *Lesothosaurus* was about the size of a chicken.

Oh no! It's Little Miss I-Know-Everything! She calls me by my real name because she knows I don't like it. Who let *you* in here, Andrea? I thought this book was for cool people.

Arlo, you know perfectly well that you and I were assigned to write this *together.* It's part of our project for the gifted and talented program, remember?

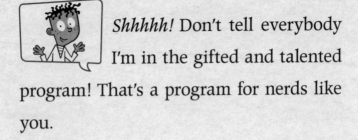 *Shhhhh!* Don't tell everybody I'm in the gifted and talented program! That's a program for nerds like you.

 Oh, Arlo, admit it. You just *pretend* you don't know things because you think it's cool to be dumb. But we both know that you're smart, and it's cool to be smart.

 Only dumbheads are smart. So nah-nah-nah boo-boo on you.

That doesn't even make sense, Arlo. Look, let's start

from the beginning. We need to tell the readers what a dinosaur is.

What?! Any dumbhead knows what a dinosaur is! A dinosaur is one of those big skeletons they have in museums.

Okay, if you won't tell them, *I'll* tell them. In a nutshell, dinosaurs were reptiles that lived millions of years ago.

Dinosaurs lived in nutshells? No way! A *T. rex* could never fit inside a nutshell.

Ignore Arlo. He just says things like that to get atten-tion. The truth is that most dinosaur species died out around sixty-five million years ago. But the descendants of one dinosaur group are still with us today.

WHAT?! There are dinosaurs alive today? Help! Lock the doors! Call 9-1-1!

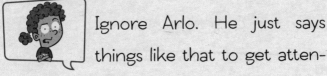I said the *descendants* of one dinosaur group are still with us today—birds.

Oh, them. Well, I'm not afraid of birds.*

 There were *lots* of different kinds of dinosaurs. Big ones. Small ones. Fat ones. Skinny ones. They dominated the earth for over 150 *million* years. Arlo, do you know what paleontology is?

 Sure I do. Everybody knows that. Paleontology is the study of pails. That's a weird thing to study. Who

---

*Not that I want them flying around inside my house or anything.

even knew there were different kinds of pails? I always thought there was just one kind.

 Arlo, will you be making silly jokes through the whole book?

 No, that's only half of the book. The other half will be toilet jokes.

 You're impossible, Arlo!

 So are you. We're fictional characters!

Paleontology is the study of the history of life. *Paleo* means "ancient" in Greek. *Onto* means "being" in Greek. And *logy* means "study" in Greek. Paleontologists try to find out about life on Earth, so they study fossils. Fossils are the remains of animals or plants that lived a long time ago. The fossils we find in rocks represent the ancestors of the animals and plants that are alive today.

Zzzzzzzzz. Oh, sorry, I dozed off there for a while. You were talking about the different kinds of pails, right?

9

Arlo, do you even have any idea why dinosaurs are called "dinosaurs"?

 Of course! It would sound weird if they were called "pot-holders."

No, Arlo! That's just silly. The truth is that for hundreds of years, scientists who discovered fossils and bones didn't realize they were looking at evidence of a whole new kind of animal. It wasn't until 1842 that a British scientist named Sir Richard Owen gave them a name. He combined *deinos*, the Greek word for "terrible," with *sauros*, which means "liz-ard" in Greek. To Sir Richard Owen, dinosaurs were "terrible lizards."

Sir Richard Owen

 What? Dino-saurs aren't lizards. That guy was a dumbhead. I had a terrible lizard once. It was called Bob.

 What was so terrible about it?

 It just sat there and didn't do anything. Then, after a few

11

weeks, we realized Bob was dead. So my dad flushed him down the toilet.

 Maybe you should have tried feeding him.

 Why? My dad gets fed every night, like the rest of my family.

Not your dad! Bob, the lizard!

 Why would we bring Bob to the dinner table?

 I give up.

 Hey, do you want to know what's *really* interesting about dinosaurs?

 I'm almost afraid to ask.

 Dinosaur poop!

Arlo, we discussed this. We're *not* going to be talking about poop and inappropriate subjects like that in this book. Remember? We're supposed to talk about dinosaurs and other animals that are no longer with us, like dodos and woolly mammoths.

Mammoths that were made out of wool? No wonder they died. I used to have a sweater made out of wool. But it was scratchy and it got a hole in it, so my mom threw it in the garbage.

Maybe that's what happened to the woolly mammoths. Their moms threw them in the garbage.

 Will you *please* stop making jokes?

 Okay, okay. I'll save them for Chapter 6. Let's be serious now. I'm Professor A.J., and I know *everything* there is to know about dinosaurs and all those other dead animals.

 Actually, you don't, Arlo. *Nobody* does. There are

many things we'll never know for certain, because there are no living dinosaurs around for scientists to study. We don't know for sure what they sounded like, or even what they looked like. Did they have feathers? Fur? How intelligent were they? We can only guess. But dinosaurs are really interesting, and scientists are always trying to figure them out. Discoveries are happening quickly, so we're learning new things every day. But we'll never know *everything* there is to know about dinosaurs unless we figure out how to go back in time and see them with our own eyes.

So if we don't know stuff about dinosaurs, we just make it up, right?

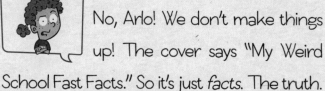 No, Arlo! We don't make things up! The cover says "My Weird School Fast Facts." So it's just *facts*. The truth.

 Okay, okay. Lighten up. Bring on the fast facts.

 But we have to ask the readers to do something too. This is going to be a team effort.

 The readers? What do *they*

17

have to do? They can just sit there and do nothing, like my lizard, Bob.

 As usual, you're wrong, Arlo. The readers have a *very* important job to do.

 What?

 They have to turn the pages, of course!*

---

*What are you looking down here for? The book is up *there*, dumbhead!

When and Where Did Dinosaurs Live?

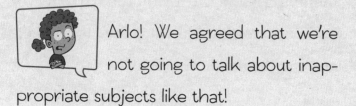

Okay, let's get down to business here. The first thing everybody needs to know about dinosaur poop is that—

Arlo! We agreed that we're not going to talk about inappropriate subjects like that!

Oh yeah, I forgot. So what is this chapter about?

 Well, I thought we should start off by talking about when and where the dinosaurs lived.

 That's obvious. *Tyrannosaurus rex* was a giant killing machine with twelve-inch-long sharp teeth, and it could run up to twenty-five miles an hour. So it could live anywhere it wanted! And if some other dinosaur was living in that place, it would have to leave or *T. rex* would chase it down the street and bite its head off.

They didn't even *have* streets back then, Arlo! It was millions of years ago. To be specific, it was between about 252 and 66 million years ago. This was called the Mesozoic era. It means time of the "middle animals."

I knew that. I was just yanking your chain. But do you know why the Mesozoic era was like a hockey game?

I give up. How could the Mesozoic era be *anything* like a hockey game?

 Both of them are divided into three periods! Ha! The Mesozoic era was made up of the Triassic, Jurassic, and Cretaceous periods.

 Wow! I'm impressed, Arlo! I thought you only knew about things like dinosaur poop.

 I do! In fact, I *doo doo*. Would you like to hear some fast facts about dinosaur poop?

No! Let's talk about the Triassic period. That was 250 to 200 million years ago.

 Ah yes, the good old days. I think my grandpa Bert was alive back then.

He was not! Back then, all the continents on Earth were part of one giant landmass that's called Pangaea. So Europe, Africa, Asia, Australia, Antarctica, and the Americas were all sort of stuck together, like a big piece of peanut brittle.

If all the land was one continent, the animals and plants living there were probably pretty much the same, right?

Right. And there were no polar ice caps. It was mostly hot and dry. Deserts covered a lot of the land. So the first dinosaurs to appear were like our current reptiles that can survive in hot climates.

Yeah, but toward the end of the Triassic period, stuff got interesting. There were giant earthquakes. Huge volcanoes erupted. *Boom! Crash!* Rock the world!

The peanut brittle, I mean Pangaea, broke into two halves, and they started to drift away from each other. The Atlantic Ocean was born.

Wow, watching a supercontinent slide away must have been *crazy*! And the dinosaurs got to see it live and in person.

Well, they got to see it before they *died*. There was a mass extinction at that time. I think it was sad that so many animals of the Triassic period died, don't you?

 If you ask me, it would be a lot

sadder if they were still around. I don't want some *T. rex* chasing me down the street trying to bite my head off.

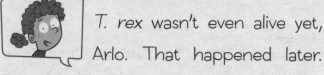 *T. rex* wasn't even alive yet, Arlo. That happened later. After the Triassic period came the Jurassic period, which was 200 to 145 million years ago. The planet got colder, but it was still warmer than it is today. There was more rain, and water covered much of the Earth.

 So the rain made it possible for trees and plants to grow, right?

 And the plants made it possible for plant-eating dinosaurs to evolve. They were called sauropods.

 Apatosaurus! Diplodocus! Brachiosaurus! Dinosaurs have cool names.

 We'll get to dinosaur names

27

later. But these were the largest animals ever to walk the Earth. By the Jurassic period, they dominated the world.

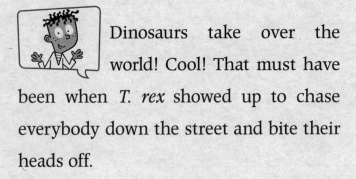 Dinosaurs take over the world! Cool! That must have been when *T. rex* showed up to chase everybody down the street and bite their heads off.

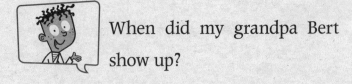 Actually, that happened during the next period, the Cretaceous period. It was 145 to 65 million years ago.

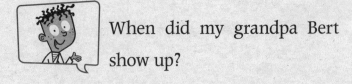 When did my grandpa Bert show up?

Not yet. During the Cretaceous period, the continents
kept drifting apart. So different kinds of
creatures evolved in different parts of the
world.

The first snakes showed up.
Snakes are cool.

Flowering plants showed up.
Insects! Bees! More flowering
plants! Modern mammals! Tree climbers!
Ground dwellers!

Everything was happening!
What a wonderful time to be
alive!

Okay, calm down, Arlo. Next we should talk about *where* the dinosaurs lived.

 I already told you. They could live anywhere they wanted. They were dinosaurs!

 You're right, in a way. Dinosaur bones have been found in just about every corner of the Earth.

The Earth has corners? I thought it was round.

 You know what I mean! Dinosaurs lived everywhere. Let's go continent by continent. You start.

 Okay, there are more dinosaur bones in North America than on any other continent. U-S-A! U-S-A! Some of the main dinosaurs of North America were the *Ankylosaurus, Diplodocus, Stegosaurus, Triceratops,* and my favorite, *Tyrannosaurus rex.*

 We haven't discovered as many dinosaurs in South America

31

as we have in North America, but South America has had some of the *oldest* ones. Some of them go back 230 million years. You may have heard of these South American dinosaurs: *Argentinosaurus, Austroraptor, Carnotaurus, Eoraptor, Giganotosaurus,* and *Megaraptor.*

Computer-generated illustration of *Argentinosaurus*

Not that many dinosaur bones have been found in Europe. That's because the dinosaurs couldn't afford to go on European vacations. But some have been found: *Balaur, Baryonyx, Cetiosaurus, Compsognathus,* and *Europasaurus.*

Africa had the oldest dinosaur found so far. It was called *Nyasasaurus parringtoni,* and it lived between 240 and 245 million years ago. Africa also had some of the most aggressive dinosaurs: *Spinosaurus, Aardonyx, Ouranosaurus, Heterodontosaurus, Suchomimus, Eocursor,* and *Afrovenator.*

Australia didn't have many dinosaurs. I guess they were killed off by the giant, evil koala bears. Just kidding! There were a few Australian dinos: *Cryolophosaurus*, *Rhoetosaurus*, *Antarctopelta*, *Muttaburrasaurus*, *Diamantinasaurus*, and *Ozraptor*.

 Dinosaurs lived all over Asia. Here are a few of them: Dilong, Dilophosaurus, Mamenchisaurus, Microraptor, Oviraptor, Shantungosaurus, and Velociraptor.

Computer-generated illustration of *Dilophosaurus*

 You wouldn't think that

34

Antarctica had *any* dinosaurs. It's so cold there. But surprise! Antarctica was warmer in dino days, so there were a bunch of them there: *Cryolophosaurus ellioti, Antarctopelta oliveroi, Glacialisaurus hammeri,* and *Trinisaura santamartaensis.*

 So dinosaurs lived all over the world. But about sixty-five million years ago, at the end of the Cretaceous period, they died out. It was the end of the Age of Reptiles and the beginning of the Age of Mammals. Do you know why the dinosaurs died, Arlo?

 Because they bit one another's heads off?

No! Do you know the *real* reason why they died off?

 Sure I do.

 Well, are you going to tell the readers?

 No.
Okay, okay, I'll tell them. But they have to read the next chapter. So nah-nah-nah boo-boo on them!

Chapter 2

The Great Mystery: Why Did the Dinosaurs Die Off?

It may be the biggest mystery in the history of the world. Suddenly, sixty-five million years ago, all the nonavian (dinosaurs not related to birds) dinosaurs died. Scientists call this mass extinction the "K-T extinction."

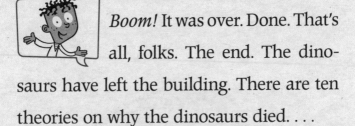 *Boom!* It was over. Done. That's all, folks. The end. The dinosaurs have left the building. There are ten theories on why the dinosaurs died. . . .

1. They bit one another's heads off.

2. They couldn't get enough food because there weren't any supermarkets.

3. They didn't wash their hands after going to the bathroom.

4. They died of boredom because video games hadn't been invented yet.

5. The Earth got much colder, and the dinosaurs went outside without putting on a coat, hat, and mittens.

6. The butler did it.

7. They went swimming without waiting a half an hour after eating.

8. They had to wait a hundred million years to go to the bathroom. And there *were* no bathrooms.

9. A *Giganotosaurus* farted and the smell killed everybody.

10. Hey, nobody lives forever.

I think those are *your* theories, Arlo. The truth is that *nobody* knows for sure why the dinosaurs died off. Scientists have been arguing about it ever since the first dinosaur bones were discovered. Some think the dinosaurs died from starvation because the larger dinosaurs needed a lot of food and ate all the vegetation. Others believe a disease spread through the dinosaur population. Others think that ash and gas shooting out of volcanoes poisoned the dinosaurs.

 Those scientists should make up their minds.

 Actually, many of them *have* made up their minds. In recent years, experts have come to believe it was a huge asteroid that killed off the dinosaurs.

 Asteroids are cool. *Boom! Crash!* Dead dinos!

 What happened was that in 1991, a big crater was found

in Mexico. It was called the Chicxulub crater because it's near the town of Chicxulub. The crater is 12 miles deep and more than 110 miles wide. An asteroid smashed into the ground there about sixty-five million years ago. That was just before the dinosaurs died out. And the impact of the asteriod released a billion times more energy than the most powerful nuclear bomb.

Boom! So the heat could have ignited wildfires all over the world.

 Yes. There would have been smoke and soot everywhere, from the fires and from the impact. The sky went dark. There were probably tsunamis, drowning everything. I bet there were shock waves and earthquakes.

 And the darkness could have lasted for months, or even *years.* With the sun blocked out, it would have been a lot colder.

 Plants would die. There was

nothing to eat. And the next thing any-body knew, the dinosaurs were all dead.

 If you ask me, that asteroid theory makes a lot of sense.

 But we can't be positive about it, because paleontologists haven't found any dinosaur fossils that are conclusively from the time when the aster-oid hit. So why did the dinosaurs die off? The answer is that nobody knows for sure.

 I still think they died from boredom because they were sitting around waiting for video games to be invented.

 That's a really weird theory, Arlo.

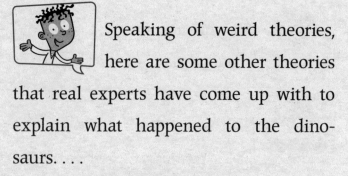 Speaking of weird theories, here are some other theories that real experts have come up with to explain what happened to the dinosaurs. . . .

In the early 1900s, many paleontologists believed the dinosaurs died because they grew too big and weird to function. I think that's also true with Andrea's brain.

 Very funny, Arlo.

In 1925, George Wieland, a paleontologist at Yale University, claimed that dinosaurs ate themselves to death. He said they ate too many dinosaur eggs. Actually, my mom has the same theory about why my dad is overweight.

In the 1960s, a scientist named Stanley Flanders claimed the dinosaurs were killed off by moths and caterpillars. No kidding! He said the moths and caterpillars ate all the plants on Earth.

In the 1970s, physicist Wallace Tucker and paleontologist

Dale Russell said a supernova exploded close to the earth and bombarded the upper atmosphere with X-rays. That made the temperature drop, and the dinosaurs couldn't handle the cold.

In 2004, a doctor named Sherman Silber claimed the dinosaurs died when volcanoes and asteroid impact caused climate change, and the skewed temperatures caused too many dinosaur eggs to be male. The males grew up and couldn't find females to mate with, so they died, sad and lonely.

I like this one best. In 2012, a British scientist named David

Wilkinson and his collaborators came up with the theory that the dinosaurs farted too much! That's right! Farts give off methane gas, and that caused global warming.

Did you hear that, Andrea! The dinosaurs died out because they farted to death! I think that guy was the greatest scientist in the history of the world. Dinosaur farts! Can you believe it?

 Okay, okay, I *get* it, Arlo. The dinosaurs farted to death. Are you happy now? Can we move on to the next chapter?

 Not yet! How do they know how old a dinosaur is?

We often hear that one dinosaur lived
seventy million years ago, or another
dinosaur lived a hundred million years

ago. But how can scientists possibly know how old a dinosaur bone is? It's not like we can look at the dinosaur's birthday cards to find out how old the dinosaur was. So how do scientists do it?

 It's almost like detective work. The way it works is they don't figure out the age of the dinosaur bones themselves. They look at the layer of rocks that was *around* the bones.

 HUH?*

---

*That's "HUH" spelled backward.

Let me explain. Do you like cake, Arlo?

 Sure! Everybody likes cake. What does that have to do with the age of a dinosaur?

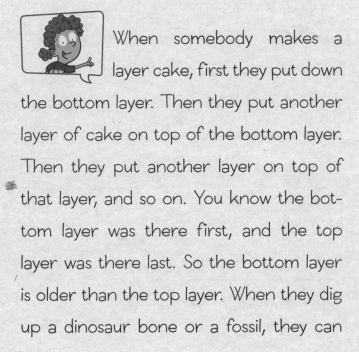 When somebody makes a layer cake, first they put down the bottom layer. Then they put another layer of cake on top of the bottom layer. Then they put another layer on top of that layer, and so on. You know the bottom layer was there first, and the top layer was there last. So the bottom layer is older than the top layer. When they dig up a dinosaur bone or a fossil, they can

tell how old it is depending on the layers of rock that are above and below it. That's called "relative dating."

Cathedral Rock in the John Day Fossil Beds National Monument

Dinosaurs went on dates with their relatives?

Very funny.

Okay, I get it. But that doesn't explain how they know how old the rock is.

 You're right. To measure that, scientists use something called "radiometric dating."

 Scientists take radios with them when they go out on dates?

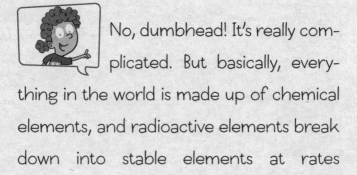 No, dumbhead! It's really complicated. But basically, everything in the world is made up of chemical elements, and radioactive elements break down into stable elements at rates

scientists can predict. It can take millions of years. By measuring how much of the stable elements are in a rock, it's possible to tell how many millions of years ago the rock had radioactive elements, which tells us how old the rock is. And then they can tell how old the dinosaur bone is.

Kinds of Dinosaurs

 In this chapter, Arlo and I are going to talk about the incredible variety of dinosaurs. Sometimes they were classified according to their diet. Arlo, do you know how we know what dinosaurs ate?

 Sure. We dug up their old restaurant menus.

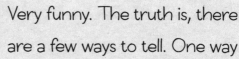 Very funny. The truth is, there are a few ways to tell. One way is to look at dinosaur teeth. That can tell us what they ate, how they got their food, and even whether they chewed it, crushed it, or just wolfed it down. Most of the dinosaurs were plant eaters, or "herbivores." They had large, flat teeth that could strip

the leaves off trees and grind up plants. They probably ate twigs and seeds too. Some scientists think they ate stones also, to help them digest their food.

 Wait. Scientists ate stones?

 No! The herbivores ate stones!

 Oh. That makes a lot more sense. It would be weird if scientists ate stones.

 Then there were the meat eaters, or "carnivores," like

Tyrannosaurus rex and *Velociraptor.* They had long, sharp, pointy, serrated teeth that were perfect for ripping flesh and crunching the bones of other dinosaurs.

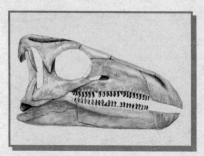 

Left: The skull of a *Scelidosaurus,* an herbivore;
Right: The tooth of a *Spinosaurus,* a carnivore

 And biting their heads off?

 I'm not sure they did that. Actually, the carnivores were not necessarily hunters. Some scientists believe they were scavengers. They'd eat the flesh of dinosaurs that died.

 Wait. Scientists would eat the flesh of dinosaurs that died?

 No! The *carnivores* would eat the flesh of dinosaurs that died!

 Oh. That's a relief. It would be weird if scientists ate dead dinosaurs.

 Then of course, there were the omnivores, like *Nothro-*

nychus, Hagryphus, Yunnanosaurus, Citipati, and *Nomingia.* They would eat plants, animals, insects, whatever.

They would eat *anything.* Sort of like Ryan. But the point is that some dinosaurs were meat eaters. Some were plant eaters. And some ate nothing but Pringles.

Okay, I made that last one up.

How did they name the dinosaurs?

The first dinosaur to get a name was *Megalosaurus,* which means "great lizard." It was named in 1824 by a British theologian named

William Buckland. Since that time, hundreds of dinosaurs have been named, usually by the person who discovered the bones or the paleontologist who figured out that they were from a dinosaur that wasn't discovered before.

Some prehistoric creatures were named after famous people. A fifty-ton whale named *Leviathan melvillei* was named after Herman Melville, the guy who wrote the novel *Moby-Dick*. *Effigia okeeffeae* was named after the painter Georgia O'Keeffe. *Diplodocus carnegii* was named after Andrew Carnegie, one of the richest men in the world. He was the person who donated money to pay for the expedition that discovered the new dinosaur.

Two American presidents have had prehistoric creatures named after them. There's a lizard named after Barack Obama (*Obamadon gracilis*) and a plant-eating ground sloth named after Thomas Jefferson (*Megalonyxx jeffersonii*).

Skeleton of a
Megalonyxx jeffersonii

A bunch of dinosaurs were named after musicians. *Aegrotocatellus jaggeri* was named after Mick Jagger of The Rolling Stones. *Barbaturex morrisoni* was named after Jim Morrison of The Doors.* *Masiakasaurus knopfleri* was named after Mark Knopfler of the band Dire Straits. Scientists must really like Lady Gaga. She has had a genus of ferns named after her (*Gaga*), a species of wasp (*Aleiodes gaga*), and a small, hoofed mammal that lived over fifty million years ago (*Gagadon minimonstrum*). That means "Lady Gaga–toothed mini-monster."

---

*He was also known as the "Lizard King."

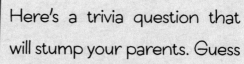 Here's a trivia question that will stump your parents. Guess who *Tianchisaurus nedegoapeferima* was named after? Give up? It was named for the cast of the movie *Jurassic Park!*

 Some dinosaurs were named after the place where they were discovered. *Utahraptor* and *Denver-saurus* were obviously named for Utah and Denver. *Albertosaurus* was found in Alberta, Canada. *Arctosaurus* was found near the Arctic Circle.

Some dinosaurs got their name because of the way

they looked. *Triceratops* means "three-horned head." *Iguanadon* has teeth like an iguana.

Here are some other dinosaur names and their meanings. . . .

NAME AND MEANING

Allosaurus Different Lizard

Apatosaurus Deceptive Lizard

Baryonyx Heavy Claw

Carnotaurus Meat-Eating Bull

Compsognathus Elegant Jaw

Corythosaurus Helmet Lizard

Euoplocephalus Well-Armored Head

Gallimimus Chicken Mimic

Giganotosaurus Gigantic Southern
Lizard

Iguanadon Iguana Tooth

Macrurosaurus Large-Tailed Lizard

Maiasaura Good Mother Lizard

Megalosaurus Great Lizard

Notoceratops Southern Horned Face

Ornithomimus Bird Mimic

Pachycephalosaurus Thick-Headed
Lizard

Plateosaurus Flat Reptile

Protoceratops First Horned Face

Saurolophus Ridged Lizard

Saurophaganax Lizard-Eating Master

Seismosaurus Earthshaking Lizard

Styracosaurus Spiked Lizard

Troodon Wounded Tooth

Tyrannosaurus Tyrant Lizard

Velociraptor Quick Plunderer

How Smart Were the Dinosaurs?

Were dinosaurs smart, or were they a bunch of dumb-heads? It's really hard to say because dinosaurs aren't around for us to give them IQ tests. And even if they *were* around, they wouldn't be able to hold a pencil. So all we can do is guess.

If you look inside a dinosaur skull, you'll see that some of them had big brains, while others had small ones. *Stegosaurus* had a brain the size of a large walnut. So it must have been a real dope. You figure that an animal with a big brain would be smarter than an animal with a small brain, right? Look at me and Andrea. Obviously, I have a large brain while Andrea's is about the size of a pea. So paleontologists would call Andrea *Peabrainosaurus*.

Artist's rendering of *Stegosaurus*

Very funny, Arlo. But let's be serious. With humans, most of what's inside our skull is our brain. But with dinosaurs, most of what was inside their skull was their jaw structure—powerful biting muscles. When scientists try to figure out which dinosaurs were the smartest, they look at the size of the brain in relation to the overall size of the dinosaur. Then they compare that to other animals that are about the same size.

Plant eaters like the sauropods, ankylosaurs, and stegosaurs were probably the least intelligent dinosaurs. Meat eaters, which had to hunt and chase their prey, are thought to have been more intelligent. The smartest dinosaurs were probably the theropods—*Velociraptor* and *Troodon*—which are related to today's birds.

 Thank you for that explanation, *Peabrainosaurus.*

The Biggest and Smallest Dinosaurs

 Dinosaurs were a lot like shoes, don't you think?

 Why do you say that, Arlo?

 They came in all different sizes. Like shoes!

 Hmmm, I guess I can't argue with that. In general, plant-eating dinosaurs were bigger than meat eaters. *T. rex* and *Giganotosaurus*, among the biggest meat eaters, were forty-five feet long and weighed seven or eight tons. But some plant-eating dinosaurs weighed a *hundred* tons.

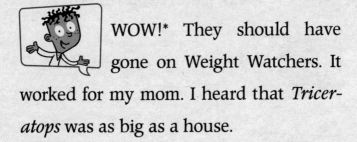 WOW!* They should have gone on Weight Watchers. It worked for my mom. I heard that *Triceratops* was as big as a house.

Actually, it was more like the size of a garbage truck— about twenty feet long. The *biggest*

---

*That's "MOM" upside down.

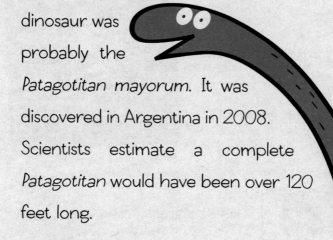

dinosaur was probably the *Patagotitan mayorum*. It was discovered in Argentina in 2008. Scientists estimate a complete *Patagotitan* would have been over 120 feet long.

 The dinosaur with the biggest *head* was *Torosaurus*. Its skull was eight feet long. And the world's biggest dinosaur footprint

was discovered recently in Australia. It was almost six feet long. Bigfoot!

Computer-generated illustration of *Torosaurus*

 The smallest dinosaur was *Lesothosaurus*. It was about the size of a big chicken. I bet it was adorable! The smallest raptor was called *Microraptor.* It was about two feet from head to tail, and it ate insects.

If you ask an evolutionary biologist, the dinosaurs never really died out. They just evolved into birds. So if that's true, the smallest dinosaur is a hummingbird. Some hummingbirds weigh about as much as a penny.

The Fastest and Slowest Dinosaurs

 Back in prehistoric times, they had dinosaur races. They were kind of like horse races, around a big track. The dinosaurs that were not racing would bet on which dinosaurs would win the race.

Arlo, you made that up, and you know it!

 Okay, okay. But dinosaur races would have been cool.

 The truth is, scientists use computer models to estimate how fast or slow dinosaurs moved. They look at footprints, the distance between strides, the shape of the foot, and the estimated leg length, based on the type of dinosaur. From that, they figured out that the slowest dinosaurs were probably the sauropodomorphs. These were huge herbivores with short legs. They didn't need to run after food because plants pretty much stay in one place, right? And because they were so big, predators didn't bother them. They moved about three miles an hour, which is about the same speed that humans walk.

 Unless we're having a bathroom emergency, of course. Then we walk a lot faster.

I'll just ignore that. Next slowest were stegosaurs and the ankylosaurs. They moved three or four miles an hour. It would have been hard to go faster than that because of their heavily armored bodies and clublike tails.

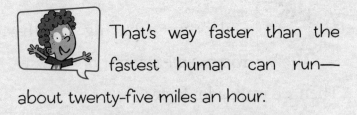 The fastest dinosaurs were probably the small carnivores that had long limbs and light bodies. *Ornithomimus* could run forty-three miles an hour.

 That's way faster than the fastest human can run— about twenty-five miles an hour.

Artist's rendering of *Ornithomimus*

So that means if we ever find a way to clone *Ornithomimus* and bring it back to life, it would chase us down the street and bite our heads off.

What Did Dinosaurs Sound Like?

Here's a fun fast fact: as far as we know, dinosaurs didn't have ears on their heads. It's true! So how did they hear? Well, paleontologists believe they had ears *inside* their heads, like birds.

Wait. Paleontologists have ears inside their heads?

You know what I mean, Arlo! Most animals make noises, and there's no reason to think dinosaurs are any different. They probably made sounds to call for a mate and to signal that there was danger or that they were hurt.

We don't know for sure what dinosaurs sounded like. Scientists have made digital scans of dinosaur skulls and blown virtual air through them to figure out what sounds those dinosaurs made.

Some scientists don't think

dinosaurs roared at all. In 2016, a team of researchers studied the sounds of two groups of animals alive today that are most like dinosaurs: birds and crocodiles. They concluded that some dinosaurs made more of a mumbling or cooing sound. That would have made them even more adorable!

Dangerous, Deadly, Diabolical Dinosaurs

I'll take this one, Andrea. While some dinosaurs wouldn't hurt a fly,* there were other dinosaurs that you definitely wouldn't

*Were there flies back in those days?

want to mess with. If they were around today, these would be on my Most Wanted list. . . .

Argentinosaurus: It weighed a hundred tons. Some of its vertebrae were six feet tall. If it couldn't sit on you, it would flick its long, whiplike tail to rip your head off.

Utahraptor: This raptor had long, curved claws that could slice you in half like a piece of cheese.

Computer-generated illustration of *Utahraptor*

Tyrannosaurus rex: Old reliable. As much as nine tons of pure muscle. It had sharp eyesight, so it could hunt you down and bite your head off with 7,800 pounds of force.*

Stegosaurus: It was slow and dopey, but it had that spiked tail called a "thagomizer." When it whipped that baby around, it could break a leg, knock out a few teeth, or bash in the skull of a hungry allosaur.

Majungasaurus: Some of their bones have the tooth marks of other *Majungasaurus* on them. You know what that means.

———————————

*Of course, it did have those pathetic little arms. So the other dinosaurs probably made fun of it.

They were cannibals! That must have made Thanksgiving dinner interesting.

Troodon: This wimpy dino had feathers and weighed only about 150 pounds. But while it was small, it had serrated teeth, a big brain, and big eyes, and it used to team up and travel in packs at night to gang up on other dinosaurs.

Could Dinosaurs Fly?

You've probably heard of pterodactyls. They were first described in 1784 by the Italian scientist Cosimo Collini. He thought the creature's wings were used to paddle in the water.

But pterodactyls could actually fly. The thing is, pterodactyls weren't dinosaurs. They were flying *reptiles*. They lived at about the same time as dinosaurs, and even went extinct around the same time; but they were *not* flying dinosaurs.

The remains of a few flying dinosaurs *have* been found. In 2007, a fossil was discovered in China that was the size of a pigeon. It was named *Yi qi,* for "strange wing." *Yi qi* had long fingers. Scientists believe these dinosaurs had skin between their fingers that enabled them to glide, like bats. There are also a few other small, light, feathered dinosaurs in the same family as *Yi qi*. They're called scansoriopterygids.

Artist's rendering of *Yi qi*

Could Dinosaurs Swim?

Back in prehistoric times,* there were books with pictures of huge dinosaurs like *Apatosaurus* and

---

*That is, before the 1970s.

Diplodocus swimming in swamps and lakes. In those days, scientists believed their bodies were so big that their legs couldn't support their weight on land.

 The scientists were so big that their legs couldn't support their weight on land?

 Not the scientists, Arlo! The dinosaurs!

 Oh. Why didn't you say so?

 Anyway, the theory was wrong. A scientist named K. A.

Kermack found that water pressure would have crushed the thorax of an underwater dinosaur and cut off its air supply.

 Ouch! That's gotta hurt.

 Most dinosaurs were land animals. When they find a dinosaur skeleton at the bottom of a lake, that doesn't mean the dinosaur lived or died there. It could have been moved there by a predator or a landslide. But most land animals can swim at least a little if they fall into water, so some dinosaurs probably could too.

In 1912, a fossil was dug up in the Egyptian desert— *Spinosaurus aegyptiacus*. It was as long as a bus and heavier than an elephant. It had flat, paddle-like feet, a seven-foot sail on its back, and nostrils on top of its crocodile-like head that would allow it to submerge underwater. Scientists believe *Spinosaurus* is the first-known dinosaur adapted for swimming.

 So I guess the answer is yes, some dinosaurs could swim. But it's not like they would be able to pass a lifesaving test or anything.

I have a question. Could dinosaurs play musical instruments?

 No! Why would you even *ask* a silly question like that? That doesn't make any sense at all!

 Well, some dinosaurs can fly, right? And it seems to me that it's a lot easier to play a musical instrument than it is to fly. My sister, Amy, can play the piano really well, but she can't fly at all. So it makes perfect sense for dinosaurs to play musical instruments. I think it would be cool to see a dinosaur play a tuba.

You're weird, Arlo.

 I'll tell you one thing that I know all dinosaurs *could* do.

 What?

 Poop!

 Arlo! We're not going to talk about dinosaur poop. That's off limits.

 You're no fun.

Chapter 4

Putting Dinosaurs Together

Before 1858, hardly anybody had even heard of dinosaurs. They weren't put on display in museums. But that summer, a fossil hunter named William Parker Foulke was on vacation in Haddonfield, New Jersey, when he heard about a nearby farmer who found some big bones out in his field. Foulke got permission to dig in the area, and ten feet below the surface he and his team uncovered more big bones. *Lots* of big bones. And it turned out that they seemed to fit together. It was an almost complete dinosaur skeleton.

The skeleton was put on display at the Academy of Sciences in Philadelphia, and it was a sensation. People came from all over to see it. The museum had to move to a larger building because of the crowds. The dinosaur was named *Hadrosaurus foulkii* in honor of William Parker Foulke. It came to be named New Jersey's state dinosaur. And today, in the center of Haddonfield, there's a full-size statue of *Hadrosaurus foulkii*. The locals call it Haddy.

Ever since William Parker Foulke's dis-covery, the public has been fascinated by dinosaurs. Scientists began searching for them all over  the United States and tried to learn all about them. What they have already learned has changed how we think about the history of our planet.

So the moral of the story is, the next time you're on vacation, keep an eye out for weird stuff you may find lying around outside. You never know what you might dig up.

How Is a Dinosaur Skeleton Put Together?

When you see a dinosaur skeleton in a museum, it's all cleaned up, set up, and posed so it almost looks like it's alive. But it didn't start out that way. It started out as a bunch of filthy bones that somebody found out in the wild.

This is what paleontologists go through before anybody can see that skeleton in a museum. First, they have to dig the bones out of the ground. After power tools and shovels clear away the bulk of the dirt, paleontologists use hand tools, dental picks, needles, and brushes to remove the rock and dirt from around the bones. This takes a long time, and they need to be *very* careful not to break anything. Remember, those bones are *millions* of years old.

 Before they can be taken out of the ground, the bones must be washed and examined to see if they need to be repaired. Some of them will be weak or cracked. Glue, fiberglass, or steel bands are used to fix broken bones.

Most of the time, the skeleton isn't complete. Some of the bones will be missing. So they have to be replaced. But how do paleontologists know

what the missing bones look like? They find out by looking at other dinosaurs of the same species. Or they'll look at other animals that exist today to see how their bones fit together. Sometimes, two partial skeletons of the same species get combined to make one complete skeleton. If that's not possible, the missing bones will be made out of wood, epoxy, or ceramic.

 Next, the bones get mounted so people can imagine what the dinosaur looked like when it was alive. Because dinosaur bones are so old and brittle, they would break if stress was put on them. So a steel structure called an "armature" is made, and the bones are attached to it with pins, bolts, or straps. Sometimes cables are hung from the ceiling to hold the skeleton up.

Finally, the museum will display information about the

dinosaur. Barriers will be placed around it to prevent people from touching it. And then the dinosaur skeleton, which had been hidden for millions of years, is ready to be viewed by the public.

American Museum of Natural History, 2015

Of course, before any of that stuff happens, the museum has to carefully measure the space where the dinosaur is going to be displayed. You can imagine how embarrassing it would be if they went through all that preparation and then the dinosaur was too big to fit in the room. Awkward!

Actually, sometimes a dinosaur skeleton gets repositioned *after* it's put on display. That's because paleontologists are always getting new information about the way dinosaurs lived.

For example, sauropods were always posed with their forty-foot neck in an S-shape so they could reach into trees to eat leaves. But in 1999, scientists using a computer model figured out that sauropods would not have been able to lift their heavy necks like that. Their backbones—the vertebrae—were too heavy. They probably kept their necks straight out and ate lower-lying plants and shrubs. Many museums rearranged their sauropod skeletons because of this new information.

How Do We Know What Dinosaurs Looked Like?

If you looked at a human skeleton, would you be able to tell what that person looked like? Of course not. Other than their height, you'd know next to nothing about them. It's the same with dinosaurs. We know what their skeletons look like. But what color was their skin? Did they even *have* skin? Maybe they had fur. Or feathers. You can't tell just by looking at bones.

A century ago, an artist named Charles R. Knight was famous for his paintings of dinosaurs. Knight combined the scientific knowledge of his day with his own imagination to create the first realistic images of prehistoric creatures. And he was legally blind! Knight's paintings were printed in books and hung in museums all over the world. Thanks to him, and to movies like *Jurassic Park*, dinosaurs have been brought to life.

Charles Knight with outdated model of *Stegosaurus*, 1899

Leaping Laelaps by Charles Knight, 1897

But how close are the dino-saurs in our imaginations to what they were really like? Thanks to the work of brilliant scientists and computer modeling, recently we've learned more about dinosaurs than we thought we would ever know.

Before the 1970s, it was hard to tell if a small skeleton was a baby dinosaur or a small adult one. But then a paleontologist named Jack Horner found thousands of fossilized eggs and embryos at a location now called Egg Mountain in Montana. That made it possible to see how dinosaurs hatched, were born, and grew up. It also became easier to figure out the age of a dinosaur skeleton when we could see what it looked like as a baby.

In 2006, farmers in China uncovered some fossils from a dinosaur that seemed to have feathers from head to tail. With that discovery and others since, scientists have determined that some dinosaurs were more birdlike than they previously thought. The evidence suggests that modern birds may even be descendants of dinosaurs.

 Other dinosaurs, we've learned, had scales instead of feathers. We know this because of the scaly skin impressions that were found in the fossils of herbivores like *Edmontosaurus* and *Saurolophus*. Other herbivores, like

Scelidosaurus, were covered in bony plates, called "osteoderms." Some had spikes and knobs.

Duck-billed hadrosaurs had grinding teeth at the back of their jaws. So they probably had big cheeks, which allowed them to hold more food in their mouths for chewing before swallowing.

What color were the dino-saurs? We'll never really know, but recently researchers have analyzed pigment found in fossils. *Sino-sauropteryx*, a small, meat-eating dinosaur, had reddish-brown stripes on its tail. The *ichthyosaur,* which was a dolphin-like marine reptile, had a very dark skin color.

 I'll tell you one thing. I wouldn't want to be a dinosaur dentist.

 There were no dinosaur dentists, Arlo!

 I know that! But if there *were* dinosaur dentists, I wouldn't want to be one. Did you know that *T. rex* had fifty or sixty thick, sharp teeth? And if the dentist hurt it, the *T. rex* might bite his head off.

That's nothing. The dinosaurs with the most teeth were the hadrosaurs. They had as many as 960 teeth! But it wouldn't be very hard to be a dentist for dinosaurs like *Gallimimus* and *Ornithomimus*. They didn't have any teeth at all.

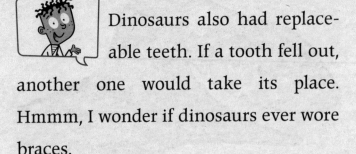

Dinosaurs also had replace-able teeth. If a tooth fell out, another one would take its place. Hmmm, I wonder if dinosaurs ever wore braces.

Here's a question that's prob-ably on everybody's lips: Did dinosaurs have lips? Pictures and movies show meat-eating theropods such as *T. rex* with its teeth bared. They're pretty scary. But Robert Reisz, a paleontologist at the University of Toronto, has chal-lenged that idea. He looked at crocodiles, which are the closest living relatives of theropod dinosaurs, and decided that theropod teeth were probably covered by scaly lips.

 These days, scientists use fossils, computer modeling, and comparisons with living creatures to get a better picture of what dinosaurs looked like. Whether or not they had lips is something we don't know for sure. I will say this—my lips are sealed.

But not with glue or anything. That would be weird.

Chapter 5

Dinosaur Doozies

In 1849, a little dinosaur called *Hypsilophodon* was discovered on an island off the coast of England. Paleontologists decided that *Hypsilophodon* lived in trees, like a large squirrel. It wasn't until 125 years later that a careful study of *Hypsilophodon*'s bones showed it had about as much chance of being able to climb a tree as an elephant did.

Artist's rendering of a *Hypsolophodon*

Scientists are only human, and humans make mistakes. In this chapter, we're going to talk about some dinosaur bloopers and blunders. But don't feel too badly about the scientists who made these bone-headed mistakes. Who knows? Maybe a hundred years from now, the scientists of the future will figure out that everything we think *today* is completely wrong.

 Why would a dinosaur have its nose on the top of its head?

There can only be one reason, right? It must have lived underwater and would pop its head up to the surface so it could breathe, sort of like a snorkel. Duh! It's so obvious!

There's only one problem. That was dead wrong.

For many years, everybody thought *Brachiosaurus*, with its forty-foot neck, lived in the sea. But now we know that

any dinosaur that big would suffocate if it went underwater. Now paleontologists believe *Brachiosaurus* was a land dweller.

 In 1923, the fossil of a new dinosaur was discovered. The interesting thing was that on the ground four inches from its skull were a bunch of eggs from *another* dinosaur, *Protoceratops*. Scientists concluded that the newly discovered dinosaur stole the eggs of the *Protoceratops*. The new dinosaur was named *Oviraptor*, which means "egg robber" in Latin.

For years after that, *Oviraptor* was described in museums and books as a no-good, underhanded, devious, not-very-nice egg wrangler who would steal the eggs of other dinosaurs and eat them.

 So it would poach their eggs? Get it? Poached eggs?

Very funny, Arlo. The truth is that the eggs that were four inches from the *Oviraptor* were later found to be *Oviraptor* eggs. So the *Oviraptor* was just *protecting* its own eggs! It didn't steal them.

 Wow! If I was an *Oviraptor*, I would get a lawyer and sue somebody.

Back in the 1800s, one of the first dinosaurs to be discovered and named was *Iguanodon*. It was a plant eater that walked on two legs. The bones were brought to a local doctor named Gideon Mantell so he could examine them. Mantell thought the skeleton would be like a giant version of the rhinoceros iguana, which has a horn, so he put the thumb at the end of its snout. What a thumbhead! So everybody thought *Iguanodon* had this thing sticking out of its face, sort of like the horn of a rhinoceros. It took decades before scientists realized that the thumb was . . . a thumb.

Kids are gonna *love* this one. When *Stegosaurus* was discovered in 1876, scientists didn't know what to make of it. It was a huge animal, but it had a brain about the size of a bird's brain. They couldn't figure out how such a big thing could be controlled by such a small brain. A paleontologist named Othniel C. Marsh came up with a theory to explain it—he said *Stegosaurus* must have had *two* brains! And get this—one of the brains was in its head, and the other brain was in its butt!

Yes, you heard that right. Marsh believed that the brain in *Stegosaurus*'s head controlled the front of its body, and

its butt brain controlled the back of its body! Hooo, that's a good one! I think that if *anybody* had a brain in his butt it was Othniel C. Marsh!

Speaking of butt brains, I think this would be the perfect time to talk about dinosaur poop. Over the years—

Arlo, we're *not* going to talk about dinosaur poop! You promised!

 Okay, okay! Chill. I won't talk about dinosaur poop.*

 Sometimes, human beings don't *just* make mistakes. They lie. They cheat. They steal. They do it for money, for fame, or for other reasons. In 1999, the National Geographic Society announced an amazing find: a half-dinosaur, half-bird skeleton that was the long-sought "missing link" between meat-eating dinosaurs and modern birds.

*Yet.

118

It was named *Archaeoraptor.* The skeleton had been dug up in China by an adventurer there.

Well, guess what? It turned out that *Archaeoraptor* was actually a fake that had been glued together from pieces of unrelated fossils. Oops! After that, people called *Archaeoraptor* the "Piltdown Chicken."

In 1845, a fossil hunter named Albert C. Koch rented a theater in New York City and charged people a quarter to see a giant fossil skeleton of a sea serpent he named *Hydrarchos*. It was billed as "Ruler of the Waters." Koch claimed he found the skeleton in Alabama, and people flocked to see it.

Unfortunately for Koch, real scientists looked at *Hydrarchos* and declared it was a fake that had been made out of ammonite

Hydrarchos in the 1846 *American Phrenological Journal and Miscellany*

shells and at least six separate prehistoric whale skeletons. Busted!

 That brings us to the Great Bone Wars.

 Bone wars? What's that? Bones had wars against each other? That must have been weird.

 No, the Great Bone Wars was a war between two rival pale-ontologists, Edward Drinker Cope and Othniel C. Marsh.

 Wait. Wasn't Marsh the guy

who thought *Stegosaurus* had a brain in
his butt?

 Yup. Cope and Marsh were
famous in the late 1800s.
Between them, the two men led to the
discovery of over 130 species of dinosaurs. But they *hated* each other. It all

started in 1868, when Marsh bribed some of Cope's hired workers to send whatever bones they found directly to Marsh. Then, in 1870, Marsh ridiculed Cope in the scientific press after it was discovered that Cope had mistakenly put the skull of an *Elasmosaurus* skeleton on its tail in his official reconstruction. After that, the two men became enemies for life.

When Marsh's crew would finish digging up a bed of fossils, Cope's crew would go to the same location and search for more. After they dug up all the fossils they could find from a site, Cope's men would dynamite the site to prevent Marsh's men from searching the area. Cope named one fossil he found *Anisonchus cophater* ("jagged-toothed Cope-hater"), because of all the "Cope-haters" who surrounded him.

The two men were constantly spying on each other, accusing each other of stealing their work. While Cope's rushed work led to careless errors, Marsh would sometimes resort to bribery or bullying to make Cope look bad. They hated each other so much that the Great Bone Wars continued after Cope and Marsh died. Cope suggested that both of their brains should be weighed to see which one was the heaviest. He was sure that his brain was heavier and that he was smarter than Marsh.

Chapter 6

Dinosaur Jokes

 That last chapter was pretty serious. So let's take a break and do some dinosaur jokes. I'll start.

Why can't you hear a pterodactyl using the bathroom?

Because the *P* is silent

 What do you call a dinosaur with one eye?

Doyouthinkhesawus

Why did the dinosaur cross the road?

Because chickens hadn't evolved yet

Why *didn't* the dinosaur cross the road?

Because there were no roads back then

What do you get when dinosaurs crash their cars?

Tyrannosaurus wrecks

What does a *Triceratops* sit on?

Its tricera-bottom

What makes more noise than an *Iguanodon*?

Two *Iguanodons*

 What do you get when you cross a pig with a dinosaur?

Jurassic Pork

 Why did the *Apatosaurus* devour the factory?

It was a plant eater.

What did dinosaurs use to make their bathroom floors?

Rep tiles

 What do you call a dinosaur with a big vocabulary?

A thesaurus

 What do hadrosaurids eat on camping trips?

Dina-smores

 How do you invite a dinosaur to lunch?

Tea, Rex?

What has three horns and four wheels?

A *Triceratops* on a skateboard

 Why did the *Diplodocus* put a bandage on its leg?

He had a dina-sore.

Where do dinosaurs go to buy birthday presents?

Toysaurus. Get it? Toys"R"Us?

 What do dinosaurs have that no other creatures have?

Baby dinosaurs

 Why did the ankylosaur catch the worm?

Because it was an early bird

 Why are there so many old dinosaur bones in museums?

Because there aren't any new dinosaur bones

What do you call a fifty-foot dinosaur that weighs a hundred tons and has carrots stuck in its ears?

Call it anything you want. It can't hear you.

 When can three dinosaurs get under an umbrella and not get wet?

When it's not raining

Which dinosaur could jump higher than a house?

All of them. Houses can't jump.

 What weighs a hundred tons and sticks to the roof of your mouth?

A peanut butter and *Argentinosaurus* sandwich.

 What do you call a one-legged *Allosaurus*?

Eileen

 How did the *Velociraptor* feel after it ate the pillow?

Down in the mouth

Why aren't there any dinosaurs around anymore?

Because their eggs stink

 How many giganotosaurs can
fit in an empty box?

One. After it gets in, the box isn't empty
anymore.

 What do you get when a
Megalosaurus blows its nose?

Out of the way

 Why don't theropods attack
people staring at them in
museums?

Because they have no guts

What do you call somebody who puts their right arm in the mouth of a *T. rex*?

Lefty

Random Cool
Dinosaur Fast Facts

Here's a trivia question you can use to stump your parents: Guess what animal is the closest relative to the *Tyrannosaurus rex*?

The chicken!

How big were dinosaur eggs?

Some were tiny, but others were as large as basketballs.

If you happen to be in a car with your family driving down Seminole Drive in Cabazon, California, don't freak out when you see a gigantic *Tyrannosaurus rex* next to an equally huge *Brontosaurus*. Dinny the Dinosaur is just a Bronto-shaped building, and Mr. Rex is just a sculpture.

Dinny the Dinosaur

 Actually, there are dinosaur statues all over the United States. You can find them in Port Orange, Florida; Cave City, Kentucky; Ossineke, Michigan; Choteau, Montana; Arizona (Holbrook, Sun Valley); and all over California (Alpine, Apple Valley, Half Moon Bay, Yermo). Those are just a few places.

 There's only one place in the world where it's legal to hunt dinosaurs: Vernal, Utah. Thousands of dino skeletons have been discovered in Utah, so in 1951 somebody got the bright idea of giving out official Dinosaur Hunting Licenses to tourists.

 Because of their size and the amount of plant fodder they had to consume, scientists think that sauropods had fermentation chambers in their stomachs, and that would have made them pass gas constantly.

Wait. So you're saying that scientists fart a lot?

 Not scientists, dumbhead! Sauropods!

 How many years did an average dinosaur live? Pale-ontologists estimate that the longest living dinosaurs could have lived to be seventy to eighty years old. That's older than my grandpa Bert!

 Some of the largest dino-saur skulls were as long as a car.

Not only that, but some cars are as long as a dinosaur skull.

 The dinosaur with the longest name is . . . I need to take a deep breath . . . *Micropachycephalosaurus*. Whew! That was a mouthful. It means "small thick-headed lizard."

 Speaking of mouthfuls, it took a *really* long time for hadrosaurs to brush their teeth in the morning. They had over a thousand of them!

 You realize, of course, Arlo, that dinosaurs didn't brush their teeth.

 Well, no wonder they became extinct. They should have used better dental hygiene.

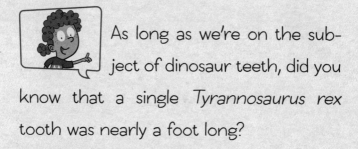 As long as we're on the subject of dinosaur teeth, did you know that a single *Tyrannosaurus rex* tooth was nearly a foot long?

 How long was a married *Tyrannosaurus rex* tooth?

The biggest plant-eating dinosaurs could eat as much as a ton of food a day. A ton! That's two thousand pounds of plants!

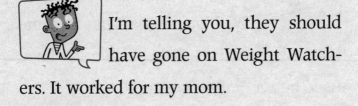 I'm telling you, they should have gone on Weight Watchers. It worked for my mom.

 Dinosaurs roamed the Earth for about 165 million years. Do you know how long humans have been around?

 Yes. We've been around ever since they started printing calendars.

 No, Arlo! Humans have only been around for two to three million years.

In museums, you see dinosaur skeletons made from hundreds of bones. But most dinosaur species are known from just a single tooth or bone.

Mary Anning was a fossil hunter who lived in England during the 1800s. She discovered the

Portrait of Mary Anning with her dog, Tray, 1842

143

fossils of a bunch of dinosaurs, like ich-
thyosaurs, plesiosaurs, and pterosaurs. In
1846, she became an honorary member
of the Geological Society of London, but
she wasn't allowed to become a regular
member. Why? Because she was a woman.
Not fair!

By the way, legend has it that Mary Anning was the inspiration for the famous tongue twister "She sells seashells by the seashore."

In 1993, Toronto was awarded an NBA team, and Canada held a nationwide contest to come up with a name for the team. Thousands of suggestions poured in, and some of the top vote-getters were Beavers, Bobcats, Dragons, Grizzlies, Hogs, Scorpions, and Tarantulas. But the winner was, of course, the Raptors. The logo of the Toronto Raptors is a dinosaur dribbling a basketball.

For many years, people in China would grind up dinosaur bones and use them to make medicine. Why? They thought the bones were from dragons!

You've heard of official state birds, state flags, and state flowers. Well, here are some official state and district dinosaurs. . . .

Arkansas *Arkansaurus fridayi*

Maryland *Astrodon johnstoni*

Missouri *Hypsibema missouriense*

New Jersey *Hadrosaurus foulkii*

Oklahoma *Acrocanthosaurus atokensis*

Texas *Paluxysaurus jonesi*

Washington, DC *Capitalsaurus*

Wyoming *Triceratops*

 Guess what married women and dinosaurs have in common?

 I give up.

Sometimes they change their names! In 1877, when the bones of a giant sauropod were found in Colorado, the species was named *Apatosaurus*. That means "deceptive lizard." Later, the name was changed to *Brontosaurus* ("thunder lizard") when some similar but larger bones were found. And then, years later, when scientists figured out that those *Brontosaurus* bones were actually adult *Apatosaurus* bones, the name was changed back to *Apatosaurus* again. As of today, scientists recognize that *Brontosaurus* is actually a distinct genus from *Apatosaurus*. Sheesh! They should make up their minds.

 When the U.S. Postal Service issued four dinosaur stamps in 1989, they got complaints because they labeled one of them "Brontosaurus" instead of "Apatosaurus."

 Speaking of *Apatosaurus*, in

1930, the Sinclair Oil Corporation started using a drawing of one (then called *Brontosaurus*) in its advertising. It was nicknamed Dino, and kids loved it. A seventy-foot-long Dino made out of fiberglass was put on display at the 1933–1934 Chicago World's Fair, the 1939–1940 New York World's Fair, and again at the 1964–1965 New York World's Fair, which drew over fifty million visitors. After touring the country, Dino retired to the Dinosaur Valley State Park in Glen Rose, Texas. You can still see him there today.

Dino at the Dinosaur Valley State Park

 Some dinosaurs were not as heavy as they looked. Why? Because most meat eaters had bones that were hollow. Birds have hollow bones too.

Dinosaurs in the Movies!

Almost as soon as movies were invented, there were dinosaur movies. The first one was called *Prehistoric Peeps* in 1905. It was based on a cartoon in the magazine *Punch*. Sadly, no copies of that movie survive today. Hey, maybe someday, somebody will dig one up, like a dinosaur!

In 1914, a silent animated movie called *Gertie the Dinosaur* was released. It's adorable, and you can watch it on YouTube. There have been lots of dinosaur movies

since then: *The Lost World* (1925), *King Kong* (1933), *Fantasia* (1940), *Journey to the Center of the Earth* (1959), *One Million B.C.* (1940), *The Land That Time Forgot* (1974), *Baby: Secret of the Lost Legend* (1985), *The Land Before Time* (1988), *Dinosaur* (2000), and *Ice Age: Dawn of the Dinosaurs* (2009).

But perhaps the most famous dinosaur movie was Steven Spielberg's *Jurassic Park* in 1993. It was based on a book about scientists who tour an island theme park filled with dinosaurs that were brought back to life from their DNA. The dinosaurs break free of the fences and start chasing the scientists around.

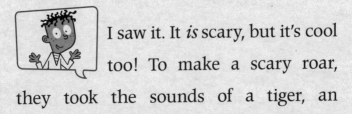 My parents won't let me watch that movie. They say it's too scary.

I saw it. It *is* scary, but it's cool too! To make a scary roar, they took the sounds of a tiger, an alligator, and some baby elephants and put them together. They made the roar of the dilophosaur by combining howler monkey howls, hawk screeches, rattlesnake hisses, and swan calls.

Dinosaurs on TV!

 It's hard to fit a big dinosaur onto a little TV screen, but it has been done. In the 1960s, one of the most popular cartoons was *The Flintstones*. It was about a prehistoric family, and they had a pet dinosaur named Dino. He was a purple-and-black Snorkasaurus.* Dino acted like a friendly dog, jumping up on Fred Flintstone's lap and licking his face. In one episode, he even did household chores like answering the phone, dusting, and ironing.

In the 1990s, there were two dinosaur shows on TV, *Barney & Friends* and *Dinosaurs*. Barney was a big, goofy purple dinosaur who would

---

*A dinosaur that never existed.

sing goofy songs, dance goofy dances, and play goofy educational games with his crew of goofy kids. Two of those kids grew up to be stars: Selena Gomez and Demi Lovato.

Dinosaurs was a sitcom that was started by Jim Henson, who created the Muppets and some Sesame Street characters. The series was about a family of dinosaurs that had evolved to the point that they did normal human stuff like go to work, wear fuzzy slippers, eat doughnuts, watch TV, and hit one another on the head with frying pans.

Well, that last one wasn't very normal.

Chapter 8

Dodos, Woolly Mammoths, and Other Extinct Animals

 Arlo, can you use the word "extinct" in a sentence?

 Sure. Somebody must have farted, because extincts in here.

Somehow I *knew* you were going to say something like that. But the word "extinct" means a species or group used to exist, but it doesn't anymore.

 I knew that. I was just yanking your chain.

Dinosaurs aren't the only animals that have become extinct. In fact, scientists think that nine out of ten species that have ever lived are now extinct.

 I know the most famous one. It's the doo-doo bird!

I think you mean the *dodo* bird.

 Hey, "do" is pronounced "doo." But have it your way. I know all about the dodos. They were cool.

 Do do tell.

 The dodo was a big bird with a large beak. It looked sort of like a giant pigeon, but it couldn't fly. What's the point of being a bird if you can't fly, right? You might as well not have wings.

Anyway, dodos lived on Mauritius, an island in the Indian Ocean off the coast of Africa. In 1598, ships from Holland showed up there, and the hungry sailors started killing the dodos and eating them. Dodos didn't even taste good, but the sailors ate them anyway. They were kind of like Ryan. They'd eat anything, even stuff that wasn't food.

The dodos were defenseless. They couldn't fly away to escape. The sailors kept right on killing them, and even the animals the sailors brought with them, like rats, cats, and

Alice meets a dodo bird in Sir John Tenniel's 1865 illustration for *Alice's Adventures in Wonderland.*

dogs, preyed on the dodos and their eggs. By 1861, the dodos were all gone. Today when people want to say a thing doesn't exist anymore, they sometimes say that it went "the way of the dodo."

 Another famous extinct animal was the woolly mammoth.

 Mammoths that were made out of wool? No wonder they became extinct. I used to have a sweater made out of wool. But it was scratchy, so—

 Arlo, you already made that joke in the beginning of the book.

I know. I thought that maybe the readers would have forgotten by now.

The woolly mammoth was a close relative of the Asian elephant, and about the same size. It had high shoulder humps and tusks that could grow up to fifteen feet long. You can tell how old a woolly mammoth was by counting the rings of its tusk. It's like counting the rings of a tree.

You still haven't told us why they were called "woolly."

 Oh, it was because of their thick, furry coat. They lived in really cold places, all over the world. Their fossils have been discovered on every continent except South America and Australia. They had two layers of fur and three inches of fat underneath to keep them warm. But I guess that wasn't enough, because a whole bunch of woolly mammoths froze to death. They were found completely frozen in ice.

 So they died out because of climate change?

Well, woolly mammoths became extinct around the end of the Pleistocene period, which ended about ten thousand years ago. Early humans had arrived by that time, and they would hunt woolly mammoths to get their fur, meat, and tusks. Not only that, there's evidence that meteorites or comets hitting the Earth really did cause extreme climate change. Scientists aren't sure if it was hunting or climate change that killed them off.

Woolly mammoth fossils at the Los Angeles County Museum of Art

Wait. Somebody's killing off scientists?!

 No! Woolly mammoths!

Woolly mammoths are killing off scientists?!

 No! Scientists aren't sure what killed off the woolly mammoths. It might have been a combination of hunting *and* climate change, maybe caused by the meteorite impact.

 Oh. Why didn't you say so?

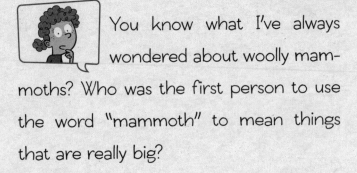
You know what I've always wondered about woolly mammoths? Who was the first person to use the word "mammoth" to mean things that are really big?

Oh, I know that one!

You do?

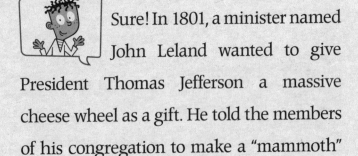
Sure! In 1801, a minister named John Leland wanted to give President Thomas Jefferson a massive cheese wheel as a gift. He told the members of his congregation to make a "mammoth"

cheese. When Jefferson received the gift, he wrote to his son-in-law to tell him about this "mammoth" cheese, and the word went down in history.

Arlo, sometimes you surprise me with how much you know.

Thank you! Besides dodos and woolly mammoths, there are lots of other extinct animals. Hey, let's make a list of our favorite animals that don't exist anymore. I'll start. Introducing . . .

A.J.'s Favorite Extinct Animals

Moa: These were giant birds

that walked along on two powerfully built legs. Some of them were taller and heavier than today's ostriches. But here's the thing. They  couldn't fly, and they didn't even have wings! Are you kidding me? Birds that didn't have wings? Are there fish that don't have gills? Centipedes that don't have legs? Octopuses that don't have tentacles? Bees that don't have knees?

 Okay, Arlo, we get it.

 **Haast's Eagle:** This was the

largest eagle in the world. Some of them weighed thirty-six pounds. They had talons as big as a tiger's claws. And you'll never believe in a million hundred years the main reason why they became extinct. Give up? It was because just about the only thing they ate were moas! So when the moas became extinct, the Haast's

eagles had nothing to eat, and they became extinct too. Sheesh! I'm a picky eater, but I'm not going to die to avoid trying new foods.

 California Grizzly Bear: Have you ever seen the state flag of California? It has a bear on it, the California grizzly bear. It's the mascot of the University of California and the UCLA Bruins. I hope nobody gets too emotionally attached to the California grizzly bear, because the last one was hunted and killed in 1922.

 Atlas Bear: During the Roman Empire, hunters traveled

to Africa and brought back these bears to be killed at gladiator events. And they say we mistreat animals *today*! The Atlas bear actually outlived the Roman Empire, so nah-nah-nah boo-boo on the Romans. But hunters got to them anyway. It wasn't until the 1870s that the Atlas bears were all gone.

Okay, Andrea. Your turn.

Andrea's Favorite Extinct Animals

Passenger Pigeon: There used to be billions of these in North America. They would travel in a group, and a flock of them was so big that it might take fourteen *hours* for it to fly by. The sky would go dark because the pigeons blocked out the sun. That's why they became extinct. They were easy to shoot out of the sky. Hunters killed them for their tasty meat, and they sold the feathers to be used to make beds. They even hunted pigeons in their nesting grounds, which kept the pigeons from reproducing enough to survive. The last passenger pigeon was named Martha. She died at the Cincinnati Zoo in 1914.

Martha, the last passenger pigeon

Short-Faced Bear: It sounds cute, huh? This bear had a

short face. It must have been adorable. But when it stood up on its hind legs, it was up to twelve feet tall! It had powerful jaws that could crush a skull. One swipe of its huge paw and it was all over for you. The short-faced bear ate as much as thirty-five pounds of meat a day. That's a lot of meat! Maybe that's why it became extinct eleven thousand years ago. It needed so much meat, and competition with other black and brown bears of the time became fierce. They didn't have butchers in those days.

Steller's Sea Cows: They weren't really cows. They were thirty-foot-long creatures in the same order as manatees, and they were discovered by a German naturalist in 1741. Soon after that, Russian seal hunters started killing them to eat on long sea journeys. Just twenty-seven years after they were discovered, they were extinct.

Rodrigues Solitaire: There once was this bird that had weird-looking things on its wings that were shaped like doorknobs. When it was threatened, the adult male Rodrigues solitaire would hit other animals with its wings. It made a sound like thunder. But I guess that didn't work very well, because they're all gone now. Maybe instead of whacking other animals, they should have just played solitaire.

Turnspit Dog: You know how meat is turned slowly over an open flame to cook it evenly on all sides? Well, back in the 1500s, some genius got the bright idea to breed dogs that would run in wheels so people wouldn't have to turn the meat themselves. They were called "turnspit dogs." They were treated almost like machines rather than like dogs. One day a week, Sunday, the dogs got the day off. They could go to church and act as foot warmers for the family. Nice life, huh?

Well, around 1900, cheap machines called clock jacks pushed turnspits out of the picture, and the turnspit dog became extinct.

Animals We've Lost in Our Lifetime

Not all animals became extinct a long time ago. These are a few of the many animals we've lost in just the last few decades. . . .

Golden Toad: This orange amphibian used to hop around the mountains of Costa Rica. Because of pollution, global warming, and skin infections, the golden toad became extinct in 1989.

Golden toad

Black-Faced Honeycreeper:
This bird used to live on the slope of a volcano in Hawaii. It was only discovered in the 1970s, but there were only three of them known to be alive by 1997. The species is believed to have gone extinct in 2004.

Gastric Brooding Frogs:
These frogs would swallow their eggs and turn their stomachs into

wombs, and their babies came out of their mouths! That's weird! They went extinct in the mid-1980s.

 Tecopa Pupfish: This was the first animal to be declared extinct under the Endangered Species Act of 1973. It lived in the Mojave Desert and began to die out when developers moved into its natural habitat. It was declared extinct in 1981.

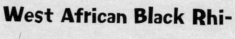 **West African Black Rhinoceros:** In Vietnam and China, some people believe the horn of the West African black rhino has special powers. So naturally, these animals were hunted down and killed for their horns. When conservationists couldn't find any black rhinos in their last remaining habitat in Cameroon, the species was declared extinct in 2013.

Baiji Dolphin: These river dolphins used to be admired in Chinese culture. But in the 1950s, the government there lifted protections on the dolphins, and soon they became victims of dangerous fishing practices and pollution. Within a few decades, there were only a few hundred left. While conservation efforts were finally made starting in the 1970s, nobody has seen a baiji dolphin since 2004.

Endangered Animals Today

The nice thing about extinct animals is that you don't have to feed them, take them to the vet, or clean up their poop.

Just kidding.

I like to joke around a lot, but I'm going to be serious for a minute here. In the history of our planet, there have been five mass extinctions, when many species have been wiped off the face of the Earth. Today, scientists say our planet is going through a sixth mass extinction. The difference is that this time it's because of *our* species. Humans are cutting down forests, burning fossil fuel and heating up the atmosphere, and polluting the oceans. Beautiful creatures are dying off.

Take tigers, for instance. Three "subspecies" of tiger have already gone extinct. There are six subspecies left. The tigers live in Asia, and there are fewer than four thousand still alive.

Why are the tigers dying off? Loss of their forest habitat is a factor, but the main reason is illegal hunting. In parts of China and Vietnam, tiger bones, skins, eyes, and other body parts are used to make medicines. One tiger carcass can be sold for fifty *thousand* dollars. So poachers—illegal hunters—will do just about anything to kill tigers.

All over the world, animal species are dying out. Sometimes it's because of hunting, sometimes there are other reasons. As we write this, there are only 109 Hawaiian crows left on the planet. Native to Brazil, there are only 130 bright blue Spix's macaws left. In Russia, near the Chinese border, the amur leopard population is

Spix's macaw

down to 349. In New Zealand, there are only 123 yellow green kakapo parrots left. The population of the national bird of the Philippines, called the Philippine eagle, is down to fewer than 500. There are fewer than 300 Sumatran rhinoceroses left in the wild.

The brown spider monkey in Colombia and Venezuela is endangered and very close to extinction. So is the Siamese crocodile in Southeast Asia. The mountain gorilla in Africa. The Arakan forest turtle in Myanmar. The Iberian lynx in Spain and Portugal. The list goes on and on. In the next century, there will be ten *billion* human beings living on planet Earth, and many other species will be

going the way of the dodo. Maybe someday ours will too.

 All this talk about extinction is
starting to make me feel sad.
I love animals!

 Maybe I can cheer you up,
Andrea. There *is* some good
news.

 Please. Let's hear it.

 There have been times when
everybody thought an animal
was extinct and then—surprise!—it showed

up. The okapi lives in Africa and looks like a cross between a giraffe and a

Okapi

zebra. For decades, scientists thought it was extinct. Then one day in 2008, a bunch of okapi were spotted hanging around a national park in the Congo!

In fact, about a third of the mammals that scientists labeled extinct were found to still be alive. They had just moved to a different habitat!

Well, that makes me feel a little better.

De-Extinction: Bringing Dead Animals Back to Life!

Scientists all over the world are working really hard to protect endangered species and even bring *back* species that have gone extinct. This isn't Frankenstein stuff. It's for *real*. In 2013, the body of a forty-thousand-year-old female woolly mammoth was found in Siberia. Frozen in the permafrost, scientists found some of her blood and muscle tissue. They're hoping to get enough DNA from these samples to clone a new woolly mammoth.

Bringing back an extinct animal isn't easy. In 2009, scientists tried to create a clone from the DNA in skin samples taken from the last Pyrenean ibex, which was declared extinct nine years earlier. Sadly, the clone only lived seven minutes and the Pyrenean ibex was extinct again.

But they're trying. So someday, we may be seeing woolly mammoths and other extinct animals again.

Hey, maybe one of *us* will be part of the effort. In 2012, an eleven-year-old Russian boy named Yevgeny Salinder was out walking his dogs. His friends called him Zhenya. Suddenly, Zhenya saw something sticking out of the ground. It turned out to be the remains of a male woolly mammoth that died about thirty thousand years ago. The mammoth was nicknamed Zhenya in honor of the boy who found it.

Do you love animals like Arlo and I do? Do you wonder what you can do to prevent them from becoming extinct? There are many organizations that fight to save endangered species. Here are a few you may want to check out with a grown-up. . . .

—World Wide Fund for Nature (WWF) wwf.panda.org

—Wildlife Conservation Society (WCS) www.wcs.org

—Sea Shepherd Conservation Society (SSCS) www.seashepherd.org

The Ending

Wow! You really impressed me in that last chapter, Arlo. I always thought you were an immature boy who just made dumb jokes and only cared about silly, disgusting things. Now I know that you're actually a sensitive human being who cares about animals and saving the lives of endangered species. I think this is the start of a new Arlo.

I think you're right, Andrea. And that means that now I can talk about prehistoric poop!*

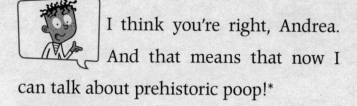 What?!

Like everybody, dinosaurs had to poop sometimes, right? And they didn't exactly clean up after themselves. In fact, dinosaur poop is still around, in fossilized form. Scientists call it "coprolite." Do you know why dinosaur poop is called coprolite, Andrea?

---

*This is my favorite chapter!

 I give up.

 Because it sounds more scientific than dinosaur poop! Actually, it comes from the Greek words *kopros*, which means "dung," and *lithikos*, which means "stone." But I like to call it dinosaur poop. And I know everything there is to know about dinosaur poop.

 I'm sure you do, Arlo.

 When I grow up, I'm going to be a paleoscatologist. That's a scientist who studies prehistoric poop.

Yes, that's a real job! A paleoscatologist named Karen Chin at the University of Colorado has been studying dinosaur poop for over twenty-five years. That's a long time to think about poop! But she says dinosaur poop can help us learn how dinosaurs interacted with each other and what the conditions were like when they lived. Isn't that interesting?

 Not to me.

 Well, maybe you'll find *this* interesting, Andrea. The largest dinosaur poop ever found was twenty-five inches long and almost seven inches wide. Wow! That was some poop! I know what you're thinking, Andrea. You're wondering which dinosaur produced a ton of poop every day?

 Actually, I was wondering when this chapter would end.

 It was the sauropod. A whole

ton! And just remember, it would be millions of years before toilets were invented. Want to hear some other fast facts about dinosaur poop?

 I can hardly wait.

 In Ipswich, England, there's a street called Coprolite Street. The street was named after dinosaur poop!

 I think I've heard enough, Arlo.

 Wait! I didn't tell you about

the dinosaur poop auction yet! In 2008, a guy from Ohio bought a pile of dinosaur poop that was 130 million years old. And he paid $960 for it!

That's fascinating, Arlo.

Not everybody can afford to spend $960 for a pile of dinosaur poop. But there's good news, Andrea! You can actually buy a piece of dinosaur poop on eBay. I kid you not! Just go to eBay and search for "coprolite" or "dinosaur poop." People sell it for just a few dollars. I bet you're happy now, huh, Andrea?

 Thrilled.

 I know what you're thinking. Why would anybody want to own a piece of dinosaur poop? Well, I'll tell you why. So they can make it into jewelry! It's true! They sell coprolite necklaces in a wide range of colors and patterns. I bet you would look good with some poop hanging around your neck, Andrea.

 I don't think so.

Then how about a dinosaur poop watch? In 2010, a Swiss watch company called Arpa made a time-piece out of hundred-million-year-old poop. You could buy one for just over $11,900.

 I think I may have to throw up now.

 Oh, really? That reminds me of something. I know this is a little off topic, but if you aren't interested in coprolite, you may be interested in regurgitalite.

 Oh no. Don't say it.

 It's dinosaur vomit! Yes, it was found in 2002. Peter Doyle of the University of Greenwich in England and Jason Wood of the Open University in Milton Keynes, England, said it was coughed up by an ichthyosaur 160 million years ago. Scientists may call it regurgitalite. But I'll tell you what I call it—Jurassic barf!

Will you look at the time? It appears as though we've run out of pages in the book.

They can always print more pages, Andrea. I have a lot more to say about dinosaur poop.

No, they can't. If the readers want to find out more, they can go online and do some research.

There are lots of books about dinosaurs and other extinct animals. I love learning new things!

 Books? Research? The L word? Ugh. Now I think *I'm* going to throw up!

Look, if you want to waste your time researching this stuff, go ahead. It's a free country. Maybe you'll dig up as many cool facts as we did. Hey, maybe you'll even dig up your own dinosaur.

But it won't be easy!

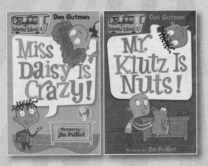